THE LITTLE BOOK OF ASSERTIVENESS

Speak up with confidence

NATHALIE MARTINEK PHD

To my husband Mark and our daughters Amelie and Isabel,

for teaching me about being a

patient and loving

communicator.

To my parents Germaine and Tibor,

for your guidance and love,

for speaking up and standing up against

abuse of power

and

for providing me with every opportunity

to live a peaceful

and

meaningful life.

ACKNOWLEDGEMENTS

This book came into being in October 2019 as a by-product of trialling a training program with medical and other professionals to develop deep listening, coaching, connection and healing communication skills aimed at helping medical professionals resolve their dilemmas and ease psychological distress. I noticed that the group was not challenging my ideas which led to the discovery that many people lack confidence or ability to assert themselves to overcome challenging situations, transform unsatisfying relationships and workplace cultures.

Assertiveness is an under utilised skill in every industry and type of relationship. Being assertive has the potential to restore peace and balance in any relationship where all people involved have a commitment to achieve shared goals.

There's a massive list of people who have supported, loved and encouraged me throughout the years. If you're reading these words and you know me well, thank you for your role and influence in my life that has been embodied in this book. This is my gift back to you.

I am grateful to Naomi Carter for all her editing, guidance, feedback and infectious enthusiasm for this book and my work. Thank you Nicole Azzopardi for nudging me to write, Katie Gridley for helping me organise my thoughts, Matangi for unwavering emotional support and Eva Migdal for being a legend and trailblazing model.

I am endlessly inspired by my teacher Sri Narayani Sakthi Amma who consistently models patience, unconditional love, compassion, mercy and peace. I've learned that assertiveness is born from a place of peace and acceptance of our desires, needs, values and choices to form meaningful, respectful, collaborative and energising connections.

INTRODUCTION

The aim of this book is to give examples of ways to express yourself assertively that align with your values, enable connection, negotiation and resolution.

You'll see descriptions of your fears about being assertive and how to address them.

You'll also see descriptions of possible beliefs and feelings others have driving their behaviour and how to respond to them effectively.

You can read this book and take it in. Or, you can use this book as a practical guide to being assertive in a range of interactions to restore a sense of control in yourself while striving for peace in a relationship.

You might see strategies and phrases in here that fit your current situation that you will want to try out. That's a fantastic outcome to reading this book and I encourage you to try it out!

The content of this book is also intended to raise awareness of early warning signs of unhealthy relationship dynamics that can escalate into harmful behaviour. The strategies here are ways to prevent escalation by drawing boundaries and negotiating a different way forward early on.

NOTE: The strategies you'll read about here are only intended for use in situations where you can reclaim a sense of control and won't make you unsafe or in danger of experiencing violence.

The strategies are not intended to be used in relationships where violence and chronic abuse are occurring because those situations require other supports to create safety or prevent further abuse.

WHAT'S INSIDE

Assertiveness

is a skill for the middle ground between

being

passive and aggressive

placating and punishing

tempered by

compassion

to rise above

disempowering conversations

situations

and

group dynamics.

WHAT IS ASSERTIVENESS?

First, I'll describe what it's not.

Assertiveness is not a way to control someone else or a situation. It doesn't use force to push back against someone else's behaviour or actions. It's not a skill to channel defiance, hostility, righteous indignation, criticism or aggression to let someone know that you disapprove of them. It's not a skill to evoke shame in another when you're feeling powerless and ashamed.

We can't balance anything out by pushing back against an extreme.

Assertiveness is a skill for the **middle ground** between being passive and aggressive, placating and punishing, tempered by **compassion** to rise above disempowering conversations, situations and group dynamics.

Assertiveness is **speaking up** and **expressing your thoughts** and ideas clearly, directly, honestly, and with **respect for others**.

Assertive communicators are able to **clearly and openly** express their needs, thoughts and ideas in a way that is respectful to themselves and others. They have the ability to express themselves without dominating, abusing, shaming or criticising others.

There's more! Assertive communication also involves **self-awareness** of one's own values, thoughts, beliefs and behaviour, and the effect they have in different relationships, environments or groups of people. Being aware of the **outcomes** one wants to achieve with others also makes assertive communication a way of expressing **accountability**.

Assertiveness harnesses several personal qualities and skills to communicate one's ideas. Knowing what you want to say to create beneficial changes in a relationship is as important as how you say it.

A LITTLE BIT ABOUT BEING ASSERTIVE

When you're being assertive you:

- appear self-confident and composed (even if you're freaking out inside)
- make and maintain eye contact
- speak clearly and positively
- speak firmly (even if you need to repeat yourself)
- speak genuinely, without sarcasm
- don't apologise or justify yourself
- take initiative to guide situations to remain purposeful
- give the same message verbally and nonverbally
- exude calm
- aim for peace

It's important to maintain a sense of calm when sharing thoughts and ideas and when receiving a response from the other person because it helps everyone feel safe. Being assertive means you can effectively communicate your values while respecting the right others have to express themselves, even if what they say is unpalatable to you.

Knowing the **outcome** you hope to achieve through sharing an idea or thought is important for being an effective communicator. Having a desired outcome that aligns with shared values and the purpose of your relationship or team's work together is what will help you structure your thought process before speaking. There will be more on this later on in the strategies section.

Building your assertiveness muscle takes time, practice, patience, motivation and support. I'm with you as you take this step.

Let's do this!

ASSERTIVENESS INTENTIONS AND GOALS

I am able to speak up and have a say.

I am able to speak up in a way that aligns with my values.

I feel positive and calm when I speak.

I do not cause pain to the other person even if I am pained by their actions or needs.

I am able to connect to shared values and goals to shift a situation beneficially.

I can assume people are out to get me and I always need to watch my back. Or, I can assume that everyone wants to support me even when the words they use seem unsupportive.

I can tune into someone's generosity of spirit and reframe anything said to me to discover that there's a supportive message in it.

I recognise our shared humanity and stand in my integrity when I am assertive.

CONNECT TO YOUR VALUES

We express our needs and values in all our relationships. Assertiveness aligns with our values to let others know what matters to us. Values can also be qualities of our personality that define how we want to show up in the world.

We express a range of values across areas of life. Examples of values are:

Attitude: reliability, commitment, perseverance, optimism, flexibility, accountability, ethically guided, joyful
Wellbeing: financial security, professional status, housing, nourishment, security, health, healing, peace, stability
Connection: authenticity, acceptance, truth, family, community, collaboration, spirituality, intimacy, inclusion, participation, honesty, respect, courage, vulnerability, love, humour, loyalty
Meaning: contribution, purpose, justice, learning, mourning, hope, beauty
Autonomy: control, freedom, self-expression, choice, creativity

Relationships are satisfying when we're connected to our values and we can express them. We can suffer when we can't or don't express our core values in our relationships.

Think about the relationships you have that are really satisfying. What are the values you express that make them satisfying?

Now, think about the relationships that aren't satisfying. What values aren't you able to express?

Which values overlap with the ones in your satisfying relationships?

These are your **core values**.

Keep them close by as we head into the next section to help you zone in on a relationship that needs your assertiveness skills.

CHOOSE A RELATIONSHIP

Be aware of a personal or professional relationship you're in that needs you to speak up.

Which core value are you unable to express in this relationship?

If you were able to express that value, what effect would it have on you? On the relationship?

If this relationship was satisfying, what could it look like?

What needs to happen from you and from the other person for the relationship to be satisfying?

If your issue is about a situation involving people, you can apply the same process to envision the ideal outcome for the situation.

So, now that you have awareness about what you want and what's important to you in this relationship, how does all this translate into assertive communication?

Keep reading!

BARRIERS TO ASSERTIVENESS

Assertiveness is easier without the barriers to speaking up. Barriers arise because of fear and shame. We don't always have the words to use in the moment, or we speak up and experience the opposite of what we want so we're unlikely to try again.

Consider that the fear is a signal that something's not right in the relationship and it's time for a positive change. Some relationships can become fertile ground for disrespect to flourish. You might already be in a relationship that has toxic levels of disrespect.

This is a reason why some of our relationships feel draining or meh. What if assertiveness is what's needed to express your core values and restore your relationship's life?

What if expressing your core values encourages others to adjust to another way of relating that aligns better with your shared values?

You're about to read some common fears and barriers to speaking up.

Pick the one that describes your feelings about this relationship or situation you're in with them. Then you'll look at the section on assertiveness strategies to pick out the strategy or process that will help you reclaim a sense of control in that relationship.

Off we go!

There's a power differential

between you and someone else

that makes you feel

unsafe

and

you fear that

speaking up

will make things worse.

There's a history of emotional manipulation

when you have spoken up in the past

and

you felt guilty

or

ashamed

as a result.

When someone

interrupts you

speaks over you

finishes your sentences

is condescending

dismissive

keeps changing the subject

disregards your knowledge

gaslights

and

needs to be right

and

you feel angry

frustrated

because you don't know how to

make it stop.

You don't know what you need

or

what's missing

except something feels off

so

you don't say anything

and

feel resentful.

You're willing to accept current conditions as

'not that bad'

or

'they could be worse'

or

'that's how it is'

or

'I can manage'

and you don't feel it's your place to question things

even though you know you'd feel at ease

if things were

different.

You're afraid of raising an issue

in a workplace

about inequality

disrespect

bad behaviour

taking time off

policy breaches

because it might affect your

professional career.

You know what you need
but the other person isn't fulfilling
your expectations
so
when you do speak up
it comes out with
anger
judgement
frustration
and
leads to conflict.

You say YES to things
before
you've taken time
to consider
if
it's a good idea
in the long run.

You're multi-passionate

and

you want to do all the things

and

before you know it

you're overwhelmed

and

feeling burned out.

You've agreed to do something

for someone else

or

take on additional work

and now you're overwhelmed

and

want to back out

but feel

that you can't.

You're worried that
speaking up
will make you seem
incompetent
unreliable
and
will let people down.

You witness injustices
and it seems
you're the only one who notices it.
You're worried that you're making too big a deal of it
and
speaking up
will make you seem
combative
uncooperative
oppositional
unreasonable
dramatic
too emotionally involved
and
making waves
unnecessarily.

There's a

BIG

elephant in the room

and

you want to raise it

but don't know

how.

You're worried about

hurting other people's feelings

or

causing anger

or

disappointment.

You're worried that
saying 'NO'
will make someone's life worse
because
you feel responsible
for
their wellbeing
or
happiness.

When you do speak up

you're seen as

aggressive

confrontational

hypersensitive

bossy

and

you don't get the results

you want.

A LITTLE PERSPECTIVE ON ASSERTIVENESS

The list you just read are the things that you might feel and fear. I have a few more things to say about assertiveness to put these feelings in perspective.

We can't please everyone, nor should it be our goal because what others feel is beyond our control. We can do our best to treat people the way we imagine they want to be treated yet it's not guaranteed that our actions will result in happiness. What is guaranteed is the satisfaction you feel when you act in your integrity.

Assertiveness can also be seen as an **early intervention** that prevents subtle forms of disrespectful behaviour from intensifying to **bullying and other forms of power abuse**.

Assertiveness transforms people from being bystanders into **upstanders** who can prevent harm.

Assertiveness is defining a **boundary** that wasn't there before or reinforcing the boundary when it's challenged, and not everyone will like that. You might feel deeply uncomfortable about this. Here's the good news – that's what trying something new to create a different outcome feels like!

Assertiveness is one half of the job. The other half is letting go of needing to be liked by everyone. The need to satisfy everyone is draining you because your energy is used to maintain an unsatisfying status quo.

Change is possible.

STRATEGIES

Now that you've identified an issue preventing assertiveness, and you have your list of your core values handy, you can use this next section to identify the corresponding strategy that could help you overcome the barrier to speaking up in the relationship or situation.

This section shows 7 strategies to communicate your needs, values and desired outcomes using visionary and strengths-based language to benefit your situation.

Which strategy is right for you?

You might be drawn to a strategy that feels the most comfortable or familiar. I invite you to consider the strategy that relates most to your fear or barrier in your situation AND also feels uncomfortable or unfamiliar. The uncomfortable strategy provides a greater possibility for relationship or personal transformation. Overall, your choice depends on your motivation, confidence and readiness for transformation.

Ready to feel liberated?

Let's do this!

When there's a clash in expectations

disrespectful behaviour

unsupportive feedback

negative ideas about you

or

the way you do things.

Here's a thought structuring framework to share your observations about their behaviour and the impact of the behaviour while owning your thoughts and feelings.

Describe the situation ("I notice...") and the effect ("I think..." I feel...")
Specify your request ("I wonder if we might...")
State the desired outcome ("then....").

Using "I" statements express ownership over your thoughts, feelings, perceptions and ideas.

Using "You" statements can be perceived as accusatory, threatening or blaming.

Examples:

*"**I notice** that when I talk about my research project/work you critique my methods/process without describing what you were looking for instead or what's working well.*
***I feel** unmotivated after these meetings because I walk away thinking I'm failing and don't know what to do differently.*
***I wonder** if instead you could describe my/our work with balance by noticing what's working well, what's being attempted and what can be done differently.*
***Then** I and others can leave these meetings feeling motivated and with a plan moving forward, and you can be certain that you're doing your best to support me/ us."*

"I notice that when I share my experience about a situation that hasn't happened to you, the conversation gets shut down. This prevents us from resolving the issue. I wonder if we might make sure that we're listening to each other's concerns and believe each other when we disclose an issue."

The elephant in the room

is so loud

that it needs

to be named.

You know there's something that's on your/everyone's mind but no one feels brave enough to break the tension. Not raising It can lead to growing resentment and more issues in the relationship. This can be anything from admissions of your own wrongdoing to what everyone is intentionally avoiding. Naming the **unspoken** can break the tension and be a relief.

Example:

"I notice the tension in the room and I wonder if I'm the only one feeling it? It feels really awkward to mention it because there are things we're not talking about that seem really important."

"Welcome back to work. While you've been away mourning the loss of 'x' I've been wondering how you're doing. I don't have the right words to say or know how I can best support you. Please know that I'm here."

"I didn't call you because I've been uncomfortable with the situation you're in as I don't know how to talk/listen to you about it. So rather than tell you that, I avoided calling you and abandoned you. I'm so sorry."

"I've been supporting your wellbeing/health/learning for a while and there's an area that doesn't seem to be changing. It seems that it's beyond the scope of my ability and it might be best for you to work with another specialist in that area."

Share observations about what was discussed, what hasn't been discussed and the discomfort permeating the space. Be inquisitive.

Example:

"We've discussed so many things about maternity leave allowance such as transition back to work, transition into leave, compensation and paternity leave so that we know the support that's in the workplace for pregnant women. I notice an awkward silence about our team member who was made redundant recently just before starting maternity leave. How does this event align with workplace policy for employees who are still here?"

When you've changed

your mind

a decision

a way of life

a way of relating

or

life's unpredictability happened

and

you want the other person to

adjust

their expectations

of you.

Share the story of where you were at when you made the promise/ decision, what's happened since, what's changed and what you need to do differently now to realign with your values using these elements:

Past: Where you were at when you first said 'yes'/made your decision, including what need I was meeting. ie share your thought processes.

Present: What's happened to you/within you that has led to the current circumstances and the impact that's had on you/your promise ie new information, change in life circumstances, new awareness.

Future: What you now need to do differently to preserve your wellbeing, realign with a core value and maintain high performance based on what you need now. ie describe the different action and the value it expresses.

Accountability: What you're prepared to do to support the other person through this change of plans and what they can do to support you. ie offer to discuss and create a transition plan.

Gratitude: For their flexibility and valuing the relationship.

"I joined this role because I wanted to develop my technical skills. The project and I have gone through some changes which has made me rethink my priorities. I'm no longer able to contribute to the work in the same way and I'd like to explore possibilities of transitioning into another role that leverages my skill set more effectively while fulfilling project goals. I'm committed to making any transition seamless and I'm grateful for you taking my request on board."

NOTE: This can also be used as an **exit strategy** to end a relationship or negotiate a new version of a relationship. Not all relationships endure the changes we each undergo and it can be compassionate to end it before resentment grows.

When something happens at work

at an appointment with any healthcare

or

other professional

that requires

self-advocacy.

Do your research first to discover your next step.

Read policies, contracts, workplace law and any legal documents that provide support for your request.

Collect evidence to support your claim ie emails, contracts, anything on paper, voice recordings, past records of similar reports and outcomes of reporting.

Know your rights as an employee, employer, in the client-practitioner or health professional-patient relationship.

Examples:

"I've had 'x' happen and I need to take 'y' time off to manage this."

"According to workplace policy, I'm entitled to 'x'. I'm prepared to discuss how to make my absence easier on the team, what can be delegated and what I can do when I get back that continues to support my wellbeing."

"Patients/clients should be respectful to staff. No one should threaten your safety at work. It's my role to ensure you're safe at work and it's time to review our policy implementation procedure to make some changes. In the meantime, let's discuss ways to support your wellbeing and what we can do right now to help you feel safe."

"I value your professional expertise about 'x' condition/issue. I need some time to continue my research to weigh up risk and benefits to my short and long term (financial/physical/mental) wellbeing before I'm ready to consider the treatment plan/course of action."

When someone says something

offensive

inaccurate

provocative

controversial

and

other things

that make you want to

react

rip their head off

defend yourself

or

fight back.

Don't. Pause. Take 3 deep breaths. Get curious. Inquire. Summarise your understanding of what they said showing appreciation for their perspective and highlighting what you see is important to them.

This makes you non-threatening and promotes a collaborative approach to problem management.

Examples:

"I'm curious about your thought process and I wonder if you're open to exploring it another way?"

"Can you tell me more about 'x'?"

"I'm not sure I share your understanding. Can you give me an example of what you mean by 'x'?"

"Something you've just said stood out for me and I want to ask you..."

"I'm noticing that most feel/believe 'x'. I have another perspective I'd like to share...."

"Can I stop and ask you 'x'?"

"Is that always true?"

"What will keep happening if you continue to see your situation this way? How else might you view it?"

"What are you using as evidence?"

"I have a different way of seeing this..."

"I'm really interested in what you just said! Please expand on that/tell me more!"

"Can you help me understand where you're coming from with regard to what you just said?"

When someone is

avoidant

doesn't fulfill agreements

or

their actions

contribute to an

unsafe

or

toxic

environment.

This is about **accountability** and holding people accountable to their agreements, promises, workplace values and policies.

Compassionately confronting someone's behaviour using **inquiry** about **cause and effect** is challenging them without rejecting them.

You can name the policy, expectation or agreement, inquire about the intention behind the behaviour and their awareness of their impact.

Examples:

"Seeing as feeling respected/any other value is important to all of us, what effect does it have on our ability to fulfil 'x' goals/purpose when you say/do what you just said/did?"

"What can we each do differently to show respect when we're feeling challenged by someone else's behaviour?"

"Can you remind me of what our purpose is here? When you say/do that, how does that enable us to fulfil our purpose?"

"It seems there's an assumption that we're all on board with what you just said about 'x'. What are the risks to achieving our goals when there's disrespectful/ biased behaviour/comments about 'x'?"

"What can we do differently to ensure we're able to uphold 'x' value/vision?"

"What support do you need to show 'quality'/'action' to make sure we all feel safe and respected?"

"Can you help me understand something? When you do/say/don't do/don't say 'x', what's your intended outcome? The actual impact of what you're doing doesn't match what you said you want to achieve. What could you/we do instead that's more likely to achieve that outcome?"

When someone tries to

change the subject

or

make something else important

as a way

to divert

from your point

or

talk about their

priorities.

They're doing that because they're feeling uncomfortable with the topic or they have different priorities that make the current topic less important. They might be changing the subject deliberately or unintentionally.

It helps to go into every conversation or meeting with an intention to keep track of the discussion points. It's a fascinating study of group dynamics and observation of who always gets a say, and who doesn't.

As soon as the discussion strays from the topic, speak up about what's just happened, acknowledge the importance of the other topic to the person and return to the current topic.

Examples:

"I can see that 'x' topic is really important to you right now. We're currently discussing 'y' as this is what we agreed on when we started this meeting. Let's continue with 'y' discussion."

"We've moved onto talking about 'x' while we've been exploring 'y'. Are we finished with talking about 'y' or do we need more time on 'y' before moving onto 'x'?"

"I notice the conversation keeps moving to 'x'. Can we flag/park it and revisit it at the end/make another time to focus on it?"

"I've mentioned before that if we went off topic again that we would stop and discuss why this keeps happening. I'm wondering what it is about this subject/ topic that seems to be off limits for you. Can you fill me in on what's happening here?"

COMMON SCENARIOS

Each person in this world has **values** and each person attempts to meet their needs and succeed in life by expressing their values in their own way. The way you express your values will look different to the way others express theirs. Appreciating what others are doing (or trying to do) to live their life can bypass the charge that occurs when people do things in ways that we don't like.

This section describes some scenarios you might encounter or witness on occasion.

I want to give you a glimpse into what's going on behind the scenes for the other person that might not be obvious in the moment but could be driving their behaviour. They often lack awareness about the impact of their actions, or they have awareness but are not ready or capable of behaving differently. Inserting a boundary by being assertive isn't condoning negative behaviour - it's being **compassionate** by giving the other person an **opportunity** to see and do something different.

Grab your list of core values. When you read these scenarios, try to pick out the way this person is expressing one of the values in your list.

How are they doing it? How do you do it differently? What's the outcome of the way they express it versus yours?

An aim of this is to inspire empathy about the person while using **assertiveness** to facilitate self-awareness, which can influence behaviour change. Another aim is to demonstrate alternative ways of responding to people's mostly unintentional attempts to dump their emotional load onto you.

How many have you witnessed?

When someone is
blaming
venting
showing aggression
or
threatening behaviour.

Where they're coming from*:

"I feel like I'm losing/lost control and it scares me. I've been part of social and cultural structure that enables me to keep reacting like this so there's little motivation for me to change how I react to my expectations not being met/ disappointment. Because of this, I lack the skill and capacity to respond to my discomfort in a safer way."

This can be a stress response to feeling unsafe coupled with a lack of insight about their feelings. They need acceptance without you taking the blame as the cause of their issue.

Option: Focus on what's important to them and us

"I see that 'x' is really important and it's upsetting when it doesn't work out as expected. There are a number of ways that 'x' can be done. You have your way, I have mine. Can we explore 'x' so we can develop a shared understanding of what works best?"

If you're being blamed for their feelings or they're venting about an issue, contain it and hand it back to them. This is non-consensual dumping and you're not obligated to take it from them.

Option: Stop them mid-vent. Then leave.

"I'm going to stop you because I can see you need something that I can't give you right now and I won't be able to help you get to the bottom of your upset."

*Note: These quotes are not intended for use as assertiveness strategies and are only intended to show a different perspective.

Disagreement
resulting in
unproductive
debate.

Where they're coming from:

"I see the world/do this important thing differently than you and others. This makes me question whether I'm right and the possibility that I could be wrong makes me feel shame. To avoid feeling the discomfort of shame, I use my energy/persuasion skills to convince you/others to see things my way. Only then will I be able to tap back into my self-worth and value."

Why do we disagree? We each see any and every situation through our own customized, unique lens evolved from many influences during our lifetime and coloured by our life experience. No two beliefs and perspectives will ever be identical because of that, no matter how hard you try.

It's a time waster and relationship buzz killer to argue about differences rather than appreciating the ways we use our resources to navigate our circumstances.

Focus on shared values or goal and describe the different ways you strive to achieve/express them:

"I see we think about/do 'x' in different ways. I'm happy with how I do it and it's great that you have a way that works best for you. There are other things that we need to prioritise and if we continue with this we won't be able to take our next step within our set time frame. What needs to happen so we can continue with the agenda?"

"It seems that 'name the value' is important to both of us. How about we discuss ways to express 'x value' that can solve this problem."

Someone is trying to control

the conversation

your behaviour

your thoughts

outcomes

using narcissistic traits like

interruption

and

gaslighting.

Where they're coming from:

"I experienced emotional wounding events early in life which made me believe that I need others to do what I want/need to maintain my comfort to survive. I'm unaware that I'm controlling as it's my normal way of being and I'm not receptive to learning any other way of relating. This way works for me because change threatens my survival."

When someone is controlling and trying to dominate the conversation, they're unable to listen to you. Do NOT share anything about yourself unless you want it picked apart. Deflect attention from you and focus on what matters to them. Show genuine interest in the way they think and what they believe. Summarise your understanding of what matters to them by naming their values. Excuse yourself and end the conversation This is validation with boundaries.

Override gaslighting by reclaiming control:

"I am the person best equipped to talk about my own thoughts and feelings." *(repeat if necessary!)*

Use inquiry to challenge the behaviour, its effect and consequences:

"When you tell me what I'm thinking and feeling and it's different from what I'm actually thinking and feeling, you're saying that you believe you know me better than I do. Is that your intention?"

"For us to continue this conversation, it's important that I get to finish my sentences without interruption or your interpretation of what I'm saying. Please listen and check your understanding."

"I notice that when I/others speak about 'x', you change the subject. This has happened (name the occasions). What happens to our ability to achieve 'name desired outcome' if we keep avoiding the topic?"

Microaggressions

such as

racist

sexist

ableist

and

other -ist comments

and

negative assumptions

that maintain

a

toxic workplace

culture.

Where they're coming from:

"I've grown up in a privileged and sheltered existence which meant I wasn't exposed to many people who are non-Caucasian/living with disability/genderfluid/ etc with professional status or education. I tend to attribute 'name group' people with other types of jobs/stations in life that don't require a strong grasp on English or with really strong accents/education because that's all I've ever been exposed to...that I noticed."

Biases are products of ignorance, shame or fear. Even intelligent, educated people have blind spots and many things they (we!) have yet to learn. It's easy to use sarcasm as a defense or to make a point while expressing disapproval, but this would be passive aggressive, not assertive.

Options:

Ignore: Pretend you didn't hear it.

Be naive: *"I'm not clear about what you mean."*

Acknowledge fear or shame: *"It can be hard to trust new people to work with/ look after you, especially if they remind you of a bad past experience."*

Change the subject: *"Can you tell me what you like about the company/hospital/ organisation/project?"*

Direct challenge: *"Sir/Ma'am/Title/Name, I'm in charge of your care/account/ case. Tell me a bit more about why you didn't think I was your 'name professional title'."*

Be an upstander: *"What is it about them that would make it seem that they couldn't speak English/do this job/manage this role?"*

Expose the shared bias + accountability. *"We all hold beliefs about people based on their appearance. We have an opportunity now to not make that mistake again by assuming that everyone here is meant to be here because they have the skill and qualifications to be here."*

When someone uses
condescending language
tries to correct you
mansplains
and
other subtle attempts to
discredit you.

Where they're coming from:

"I'm pressured to play into the expected male/expert role of dominance by proving my intellect, especially when I feel intimidated or insecure about what I know compared to the brain trust in the room/online. The only way I know how to ease my discomfort is to undermine the women/other person so I can (re)claim my position as an authority in the room. This is what I'm conditioned to do to prove that I belong."

Respond by retelling what just happened and/or inquire about perceptions:

"You've repeated everything I just said using different words to show your intelligence (in front of everyone). No doubt you're bright and there's plenty of space for each of us to be bright together without needing to undermine a colleague by explaining my/her/their own research back to me/her/them."

"You sound like you have a good grasp of my research/area of expertise. What do you think should be done next to extend knowledge on the subject?"

"You said several things that sound really clever. I want to make sure I understand what you mean. Can you give some examples from your experience of how you would apply what you just said?"

"What is it about me that makes you believe that I don't belong here/can't manage this role/need your approval?"

"I noticed that when you said that/'repeat the statement' to the client/ patient they looked uncomfortable and it made the space awkward. Is this helping them earn our trust?"

When a colleague or employee
who is male
is described as 'great'
and
the female as 'aggressive'
for better performance
and
you've had enough of
misogyny.

Where they're coming from:

"I've internalized cultural narratives that have lower expectations for male performance because I naturally assume they can perform the task whereas I'm still skeptical about women's performance because women doing things independently is still a relatively new concept to process. So rather than acknowledge the quality of her work and encourage equality, I have higher expectations so it's harder for her to make men/me look bad."

Challenge someone's thinking while avoiding activating unhelpful male fragility or internalized bias in women that protect men:

"I notice that Sheila puts up her hand every time we need extra help while Shawn only comes for his shifts. I also see that she's described as 'aggressive', 'sensitive' or 'bossy' when she shows initiative and suggests ways to make processes more efficient while Shawn is described as reliable and a go getter for performing his tasks as required, nothing more. This is a glaring difference in perception of performance and I wonder what impact that has on the performance of both Sheila and Shawn if this difference continues?"

"Have you heard the term 'unconscious bias'? I'm bringing this up now because I want to know if the phenomenon is occurring here among us and that's why we can't retain women?"

"I notice that when you talk about the men in the group, it's with a fondness as if you're their protector. When you talk about the women in the group, you have a different way of talking about them that's distant/detached. Are you aware you're doing that? What 's your thinking/motivation behind doing that?"

A LITTLE PEP TALK TO MOTIVATE ACTION

There's struggle in not having the words to say in the heat of the moment.

You're going to feel really uncomfortable, afraid of rejection, abandonment and all the bad things in the moment when the opportunity for assertiveness presents itself.

But what if trying something different can break you and that person out of the disempowering relating cycle into another way?

What about striving for the best outcome rather than striving to avoid the worst one?

Can the feeling of peace that arises from acting in your integrity be a motivator to being compassionately assertive?

What if doing this is preventing the abuse of someone else?

It might take time to develop your own script and language use. Then there's a process of building confidence to use the phrase.

You'll have to rehearse it in your mind a few times or role play with trusted supports in your life.

You might try to use it and it'll be in the wrong place at the wrong time. Don't be discouraged! Every time you aim for peace, resolution and the best possible outcome you're flexing your assertiveness muscle until it's strong and powerful!

Eventually assertiveness will come out at the right place, right time in the right way.

Keep up the intention, vision and effort and shift will happen!

REFERENCES

Dale Carnegie Training. (2009). The 5 essential people skills: how to assert yourself, listen to others, and resolve conflicts. New York: Simon & Schuster.

Day, C., Ellis, M., & Harris, L. (2014). Family Partnership Model. Reflective Practice Handbook.

Facilitating weekly meditation sessions for hospital and research institute staff for 4 years that hones in on the group's core issue, needs and best possible reality.

Group facilitation using partnership-centred practice followed by reflective practice sessions with my mentors and supervisors using the Working in Partnership Model. Thank you Dr. Paul Prichard, Martin O'Byrne, Donna Anderson, Deb Sestak and Leonie Symes. You are masterful facilitators.

Mediation and dispute resolution training and practice for 3 years.

Application of all the scripts in this book in my work with clients and learning from their experience. Application of these scripts in my own life and learning from the outcomes of every attempt to inform my next attempt.

Witnessing and analysing healthcare cultures and relationship dynamics that maintain power imbalance as well as level the playing field.

Hundreds of conversations with diverse health professionals, trainees and students about their experiences of education, training and practice, discovering overlapping themes and patterns that lead to or protect from burnout and empathy drain.

Trialling these ideas with the Safe Space Health community and receiving feedback.

A LITTLE ABOUT THE AUTHOR

I'm Nathalie!

Our species is experiencing a burnout epidemic. We're stuck in conflict, blame, shame and so many not so fab experiences. There are many reasons for this which means there are many fixes and prevention strategies. I chose to zone in on assertiveness because I see a deficit in this skill that's hurting the way we relate to each other.

I've been observing human behaviour in all types of relationships for years. I see patterns in the way people react, speak and relate to others when they feel challenged, scared, shame and other uncomfortable feelings that are effective for disconnection, otherizing and unresolving conflict.

I've learned that there are many conversations that are being avoided and so many more that people don't even know they need to have as part of a relationship maintenance effort. We suffer because of what remains unsaid.

So this is my bit to help people have the words and statements they need to bypass power games and bring a little peace and harmony into their relationships.

I'm a human connection specialist and relationship coach. I help people translate their feelings, needs, values, desires and vision into words to promote peace, healing and resolution within themselves and in their relationships. I use a variety of transformative approaches to dismantle power structures that cause suffering and renovate relationship dynamics that support safety, respect, trust, honesty, peace, accountabliity and all the things we all value for a fulfilling life.

There's more! Check me out at **drnathaliemartinek.com**

Being compassionate

is

speaking up about

negative behaviour

while giving the other person

an opportunity

to see and do

something different.

Assertiveness

is a skill

for expressing

compassion

using words.

About the cover image:

This photo makes a statement about how our boundaries, facilitated by assertiveness, can prevent negativity and people's emotional load from infiltrating our own space.

Water also represents our emotions and the ocean represents the breadth and depth of emotional and human experience. When we draw a line in the sand it's because we want to have healthy boundaries that ensure personal safety and wellbeing. The wave didn't go past the line drawn in the sand.

This was symbolic that our inner strength and healthy boundaries can support us to witness other people's emotional states without being disturbed, reactive or drowned by it. We can better assist someone and handle any intense situation when we stay dry.

www.ingramcontent.com/pod-product-compliance
Lightning Source LLC
Chambersburg PA
CBHW080254030426
42334CB00023BA/2819